PRIPYAT

THE CHERNOBYL GHOST TOWN

BY LISA OWINGS

BELLWETHER MEDIA, MINNEAPOLIS, MN

Are you ready to take it to the extreme?
Torque books thrust you into the action-packed world
of sports, vehicles, mystery, and adventure. These
books may include dirt, smoke, fire, and chilling tales.
WARNING: read at your own risk.

This edition first published in 2018 by Bellwether Media, Inc.

No part of this publication may be reproduced in whole or in part without written permission of the publisher. For information regarding permission, write to Bellwether Media, Inc., Attention: Permissions Department, 5357 Penn Avenue South, Minneapolis, MN 55419.

Library of Congress Cataloging-in-Publication Data

Names: Owings, Lisa, author.
Title: Pripyat : The Chernobyl Ghost Town / by Lisa Owings.
Description: Minneapolis, MN : Bellwether Media, Inc., [2018] | Series:
   Torque. Abandoned Places | Includes bibliographical references and index.
   | Audience: Ages 7-12. | Audience: Grades 3-7.
Identifiers: LCCN 2016059011 (print) | LCCN 2016059896 (ebook) | ISBN
   9781626176973 (hardcover : alk. paper) | ISBN 9781681034270 (ebook)
Subjects: LCSH: Chernobyl Nuclear Accident, Chornobyl', Ukraine,
   1986–Juvenile literature. | Pryp'iat' (Ukraine)–History–20th
   century–Juvenile literature.
Classification: LCC TK1362.U38 O95 2017 (print) | LCC TK1362.U38 (ebook) |
   DDC 363.47/99094777–dc23
LC record available at https://lccn.loc.gov/2016059011

Editor: Betsy Rathburn   Designer: Brittany McIntosh

Printed in the United States of America, North Mankato, MN.

TABLE OF CONTENTS

ENTER AT
YOUR OWN RISK

Your stomach turns as the tour van nears the city of Pripyat. **Radiation** warning signs flash past your window. **Geiger counters** chirp their findings. Is this really safe?

You ignore your fears and climb off the bus. You step over **rubble**, looking up at the weathered buildings. They have stood empty for more than 30 years.

Paint peels from a hotel's crumbling walls. A swimming pool holds nothing but broken tile. A rusted Ferris wheel rises over a silent amusement park.

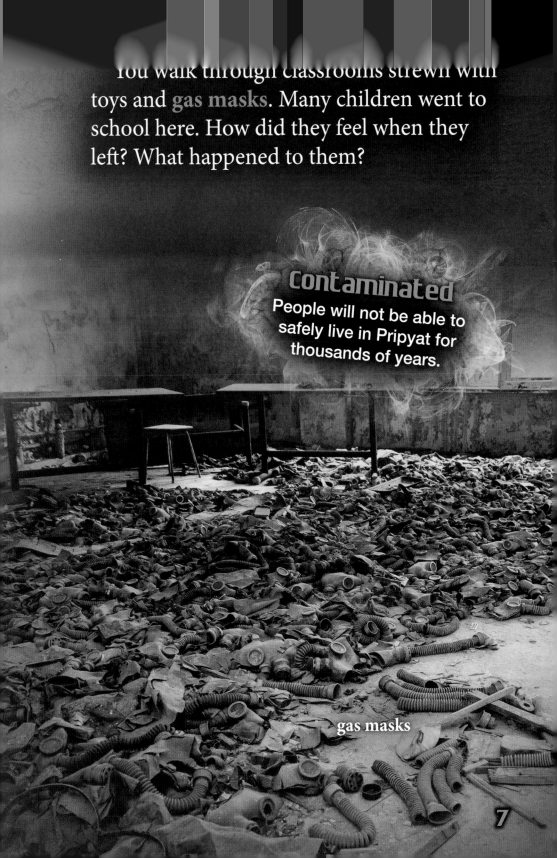

You walk through classrooms strewn with toys and **gas masks**. Many children went to school here. How did they feel when they left? What happened to them?

contaminated
People will not be able to safely live in Pripyat for thousands of years.

gas masks

THE NINTH NUCLEAR CITY

Pripyat is a city in the Eastern European country of Ukraine. It lies near Ukraine's northern border. When it was built, Pripyat was part of the Soviet Union.

The town became the Soviet Union's ninth nuclear city. It supported the Chernobyl Nuclear Power Plant about 2 miles (3 kilometers) away. People moved to Pripyat to work at the plant.

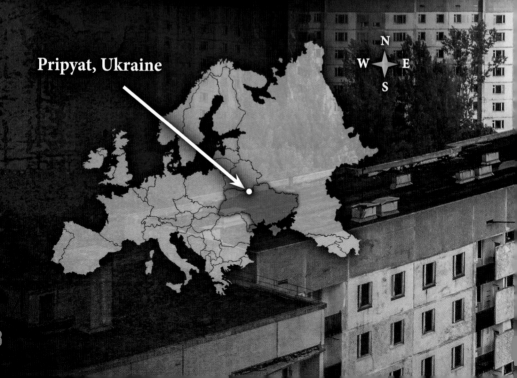

Pripyat, Ukraine

N
W · E
S

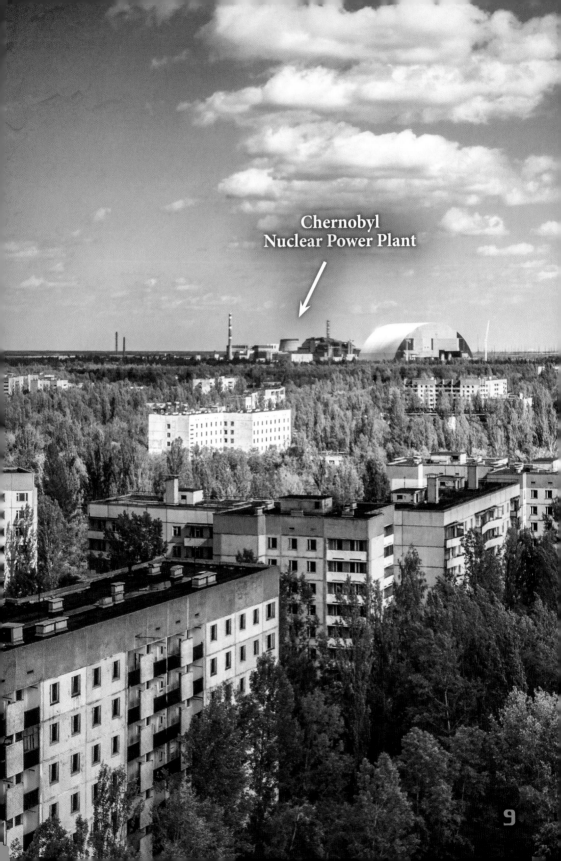

Chernobyl
Nuclear Power Plant

Mostly young people lived and worked in Pripyat. The average age was 26. Many of the townspeople had young children.

The Soviet government praised nuclear power as safe and modern. Few special measures were taken to protect Pripyat from possible dangers. No one was prepared for what was to come.

A Powerful Dream

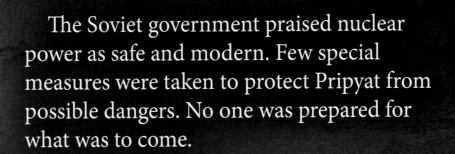

Supporters believed nuclear power could provide unlimited energy. They thought it would make the world a better place.

PRIPYAT, BEFORE

Pripyat was founded on February 4, 1970. It became the closest city to the Chernobyl Nuclear Power Plant. Workers and their families filled the town. They believed the power plant would bring great **prosperity**.

As Pripyat grew, the plant was still being built. It opened when its first **nuclear reactor** was finished in 1977.

By 1979, Pripyat was blossoming.
The population swelled to almost 50,000 by
1986. Schools, shops, and theaters opened
to serve the needs of the growing city.

Meanwhile, three more reactors had been built at Chernobyl. Some workers warned of problems that made the plant unsafe. Sadly, few took them seriously.

Broken Promises
Ukraine's government boasted about Chernobyl's safety. They said it could run for 10,000 years without failure.

PRIPYAT TIMELINE

1970:
Pripyat is founded

1979:
Pripyat officially
becomes a city

1977:
Chernobyl Nuclear
Power Plant opens

1983:
The fourth reactor at
Chernobyl is completed

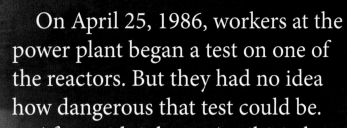

On April 25, 1986, workers at the power plant began a test on one of the reactors. But they had no idea how dangerous that test could be.

After midnight on April 26, the reactor became unstable. The team struggled to gain control. One worker tried to stop the test. Still, they kept going.

1986:
A Chernobyl reactor explodes, and Pripyat is abandoned

2000:
Chernobyl's last reactor is shut down

DISASTER AT CHERNOBYL

The workers made a series of mistakes. The test soon spiraled out of control. At 1:23 a.m. on April 26, the reactor exploded.

Radiation Sickness

Nuclear radiation can be very harmful. It damages cells in the body. People exposed to high doses get very sick and may die. Lower doses may cause cancer years later.

Radiation drifted through the air. It would later rain down on a huge area from Europe to Asia. Emergency workers rushed to contain the damage. Many of those at the scene that day received deadly doses of radiation.

Signs of Life

After the accident, radiation made it hard for plants and animals to stay healthy. Today, the area is much safer for wildlife.

On April 27, the people of Pripyat had only two hours to gather their things. Then buses arrived to take them to safety. No one would return.

More than 30 people were killed immediately after the accident. Many more have since died or fallen ill. Only time will tell the full effects of the disaster.

GLOSSARY

gas masks—masks used to filter harmful gases and materials out of the air to make it safe to breathe

Geiger counters—devices that measure radiation levels

nuclear city—a type of closed city where only certain people are allowed to live; nuclear cities were built to support nuclear power plants.

nuclear power—a type of power that burns no fuel; nuclear power plants use nuclear power to make electricity.

nuclear reactor—a large structure in which nuclear reactions release energy

prosperity—success and wealth

radiation—a type of energy produced by radioactive substances and nuclear reactions; radiation can be dangerous or helpful.

rubble—broken pieces of brick, stone, or other materials from a fallen building

Soviet Union—short for the Union of Soviet Socialist Republics, a former country made up of 15 republics or states, including Ukraine

TO LEARN MORE

AT THE LIBRARY

Borgert-Spaniol, Megan. *Ukraine*. Minneapolis, Minn.:
Bellwether Media, Inc., 2014.

Rissman, Rebecca. *The Chernobyl Disaster*. Minneapolis,
Minn.: ABDO Publishing Company, 2014.

Spilsbury, Richard and Louise. *Nuclear Power*.
New York, N.Y.: PowerKids Press, 2012.

ON THE WEB

Learning more about Pripyat
is as easy as 1, 2, 3.

1. Go to www.factsurfer.com.

2. Enter "Pripyat" into the search box.

3. Click the "Surf" button and you will see a list of
related web sites.

With factsurfer.com, finding more information
is just a click away.

INDEX